LINGER, LOVE.

Poems by Liz Shine

Illustrated by Emelita Trier

Copyright © 2016 by Liz Shine

All rights reserved. This book or any portion thereof may not be reproduced or used in any manner whatsoever without the express written permission of the publisher except for the use of brief quotations in a book review.

Printed in the United States of America

First Printing, 2016

ISBN 978-0-9974670-0-0
Red Dress Press
www.lizshine.com

For Winston.

ACKNOWLEDGMENTS

"Poppies in May" was published in the Writer's Ezine in 2002 and can no longer be found online. "Linger, love." appeared in 2016 in Dual Coast Magazine.

Poems were my gateway into a writing life. I've collected some poems written over time here in this colllection as a sort of essay on the human heart. For these poems and all the others, I have so many people to thank. Dr. Carter who gave me a voice in Senior English. Danielle, who sat with me at the cemetary reading from *Leaves of Grass.* Aunts Carol and Jimi who encouraged me in my writing by buying me books about writing. Aunt Sue who insisted I write my feelings down. My brother, Nate, who jumped right in with me. My sister, who illustrated this book and helped me with InDesign. Carrie, who encourages me to write every day. Chris, my wonder partner-in-crime. My mother, who raised me in a lyrical home. Natalie and Kristina, and all my writer friends who continue to explore this writing life with me, who read my work and help me get better. My son, whom I dedicate this book to, for his inspiring kindness and generosity. Namaste.

CONTENTS

Sips	9
Anjo's Quickstop	10
Puyallup Fair, 1979	11
Memory	12
Pants on Fire	13
Stars	14
Thou Shalt Not	15
Winged	16
Chemistry	17
A poet's influence, a la Ginsberg	18-19
Portland	20
Granny	21
Hummus	22
In The Kitchen	23
Moon Walk	24-25
Epiphany of a young mother	26-27
Get Home Soon	28
Love	29
Ladies, love!	30
Pecan Pie	31
A Grape. A Worm. A Kaleidoscope.	32
What I Learned From The Rain	33
Pay Day	34
Obstinate	35
Sunset In That Lonesome Valley	36
Mat	37
Love letter	38
Bankrupt	39
Balboa Park	40-41
Loneliness	42-43
Even In Silence	44
Enchanted Valley	45

Open Space	46
Until You	47
Poppies In May	48
The Scultptor	49
Ode to the Avocado	50
Linger, love.	51
Language	52
A Good Snow	53
Like the first kiss	54-55
Advice From A Swingset	56

Sips

Late 1980s,
wine coolers were the thang.
Super-cool,
like our tapered jeans, banana clips,
Tropical Sunset sips.

Neon and lace night,
tipping bottles back, getting soused,
looking to get kissed.

Can I forgive
being roused at three AM time and again? Forgive
slurred promises, accusations that I just didn't care
enough? Forgive Mom's wilting me with her sweet-rot
breath? Forgive Dad's drunk tank phone calls,
his need to be always the center of things?

I see how innocently it all begins,
then I can.

Anjo's Quickstop
(Hoquiam)

Penny candy by the bag: nickel hats, swedish fish.
On richer days: fat, seasoned potato wedges,
two tablespoon-sized tubs of sour cream.
Pac-man for two quarters a game.

My older cousin De-bor-ah,
helped me forge notes
for two packs of Copenhagen--one for her, one for me--
and then again when her mother was "too sick
 to make it to the store".

We smoked a soft-pack of Marlboros under the bridge,
in front of the skating rink,
talking about how much fun De-bor-ah
would have in middle school come fall.

Only eleven, so jealous.

Puyallup Fair, 1979

Eating a granny smith wrapped in stringy caramel,
wearing my spray-painted cowgirl hat,
counting the number of soft yellow chicks in the wire cage.
Wandering, weaving through the crowd of people,
bumping shoulders,
nodding hello to smiling faces.

I'd tossed all the dimes I had, won an ashtray,
when a strange woman
grabbed my arm, crouched down eye-to-eye, and asked,
"Are you lost, little girl?"

She took me to the lost booth
where I sat alone for what seemed like forever
waiting to be found.

Memory

Under the tree,
among dandelions and grass,
tall, cherry-ripe shade blocks the hot-bright sun.

Neighbor girls, my older brother rejoice
—no adults.
Fingers stained purple chase me.
A brother's laugh, the familiar wheeze,
my own watering hay fever eyes.

What reminds me now?
A cherry-stained Dr. Seuss book
found at the bottom of a box
while clearing out
Mother's collections of things.

Under the tree,
among dandelions and grass,
tall, cherry-ripe shade blocked the hot-bright sun.

Pants on fire

What could I do but lie?
Mad as she was,
her face distorted — red,
her tone sunk, a penny in water,
without a wish.
The lie popped out,
a last-ditch, no way this is gonna work
fight or flight half truth.

Thus began the process
that has me now fork-tongued and rattled,
waiting to be stroked and admired.

Stars

Cold sand between my toes,
I run toward the night waves.
Cousin companion follow in this
late-August family time.

We are both yelling and in this
star-studded ocean night,
we are cradled.

Soon there will be dull September days of hopscotch,
designer blue jeans, and social studies text books.
A crowd of girls in fingerless lace gloves will sing
I am a material girl, swinging their hips in unison.
But this night there are only two sweatshirt girls,
teasing a dangerous sea. Discovering that at night
there are stars in the sand and each cartwheel
sends them hurtling to the sky.

Thou Shalt Not

Thou shalt not lust
after the bold, blond preacher's son,
though he plays Joseph to thy Mary.

Backstage (really a dark closet),
lights-out, holding hands, his mother's breath
finds ye in the dark where her eyes cannot.

Ye eat ham and cream cheese Yule logs
to feed the fire in thy belly. Thou shalt not.
But tis the season to suck sugar candies, chew chocolate crèmes,
be merry. Merry, thy mind jangles.
Thy heart, a sleigh bell, a piece of ribbon candy, unfurls.

In a black room crammed with shepherds, angels,
a baby's doll, and his mother's breath,
he placed his hand on thy hipbone,
pulled ye toward him and stole thou shalt not
from where it stuck on thy tongue.

His lips met thine right before ye stepped onto the stage
amidst the falling snow (really laundry detergent)
that made you think of laundry folding day,
you folding towels just as taught,
mother's iron hissing at each new piece of clothing.

Some days later, sitting across from thy proud mother's eyes,
thy steady gaze sure, crunching New Year lumpia,
piece after piece, slurping pancit noodles,
Mother eyes speak: *What is it thou hast done?*
She knows, somehow, that this day indeed
marks a new, kissed, year.

Winged

Hot sun beats on public pool concrete.
The rules: No running; No diving; No street clothes.

Plump red-faced boy cannonballs
in the shallow end, sending a pig-tailed toddler
flailing, water-winged arms, a frightened bird,
into her father's hairy chest.

Overhead, an airplane buzzes.
All eyes lift skyward, catching
gray undercarriage, trailing white clouds.

Pink bikini-clad teen,
new breasts out, imagines she's flying that plane,
tipping her wing to spell out her name,
as she glances full circle, then dives into cold chlorine water,
feels the rush of daring.

A huddle of concerned children
carry a tiny finch to the first adult who might ease their fear.
Broken wing, found in the oleander bush.
They want to know:
Can someone help this little bird fly?

Chemistry

What is fluorocarbon?
Can't recall the precise
definition Mr. P penned
on the green chalkboard.
Know that fluoro has to do with--
flowers? Know that carbon
= building block of life.
I tried to pay attention.

Wonder: If I sat in class picking my teeth with a pirate knife--
Would Mr. P flinch?
If a tall dark Spaniard waltzed into class
holding a tarnished skeleton key--
would there be a blip in his cardio-graph?
Would he drop his acetic acid
or misspell Pasternak?

A poet's influence, a la Ginsberg

What thoughts I had of you, e.e. cummings,
as I walked a few residential blocks to the westside co-op,
sun kneading my knotted shoulders,
dreaming of the fresh-baked loaf of rosemary bread and cheese
I craved for a solitary picnic.

Vegans in the clearance bin!
Radicals in the kale!
Humans trying to be good, pulling out jars and bags
brought from home to gather their hearts' desires.

I saw you, e.e. cummings, love addict, juggling eggs,
a smile on your face, and the crowd
gathered around you singing love songs.

College students in the tofu bin!
Families grinding peanut butter!

Edward Estlin, I heard the questions you fired at the crowd —
one for each egg you tossed in the air.
What else is a heart for?
What better time than now?

Contemplating this, I turned my cart into the next aisle,
where I spied Elizabeth Bishop taking photographs of people,
then pretending, when they turned to question her, to count apples,
brooding expression settled on her brow.

And Mr. Ginsberg, I stood behind you in line,
listened to you howl for the volunteer cashier,
who snorted and laughed, asked you to sign
his environmental textbook.

When I exited the store,
My reusable bags too full because I have no knack
for finite space, you were reading the community bulletin board,
jotting phrases down in your pocket-sized notebook.

I walked home, alone, thinking,
O Me! O Love!
In the bird's songs, the sound of my sandals
tapping on the pavement,
feather breeze on bare legs,
I heard you whisper:
You are here — life exists, and identity;
who pays any attention to the syntax of things?

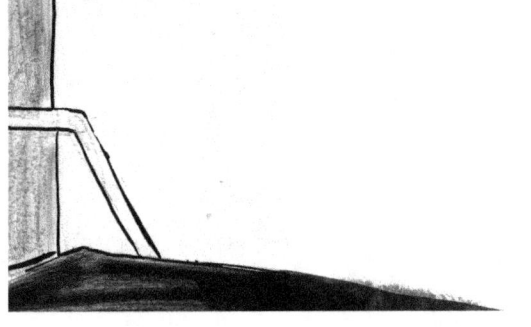

Portland

When I say Portland is a great city
(which I say at nearly every mention),
I don't just mean bus signs are color and symbol coded,
thus easier to follow, or that the fare is cheap,
or that, "It's a great walking city."

I don't just mean P-town is a publishing Mecca,
a liberal hoe-down where you can let it all hang out,
the city of roses and so many books,
saxophones, and coffee shops.

When I say Portland is a great city,
I'm talking about being nineteen,
and terribly anxious
to get to the heart
of any matter.

Granny

He was a neighbor
in a city where walls touch
walls and
houses huddle,
like campers trying to keep warm.

In the picture of the two of you,
you don't look like a Granny,
but the expression is the same,
"Challenge me — I dare you."
And he doesn't care to challenge,
his face smiling,
the way he leans on his cane, easy,
only the body stricken by polio, not the grin.

Even when the tone was scolding,
I listened carefully for your words, Granny.
I should have written them down
on these 3 x 5 cards, instead of your recipes,
because I am still hungry,
even after your five cup salad,
your lasagna,
your creamed peas.

Hummus

I learned to make hummus
while camping in an Arizona-cheap motel
with you, baby, and a half gone gallon of gin.

Under the starry cactus sky
we might have stumbled forever,
but the clinic nurse walked in
waving a Congratulations sigh.

Whoa—all I wanted was some birth control.

I brush the spinach stems into the sink,
the smell of cumin on my hands,
beans simmering on the electric stove.

Rain pounds the window.
Evergreens muffle the sound
of log trucks passing on 101,
the path of leaving, even yours.

In the Kitchen

Look for her in the kitchen
when she's angry.
She is there—
stacking the dirty dishes,
guiding the soggy rice, broccoli, juicemilk sludge
into the garbage disposal,
preparing the sink to receive the dirty dishes.

Jazz, loud enough to drown
her thoughts in hot suds.
Scouring counters, burner rims, cupboard doors.
The waxed flour sends light back toward the ceiling
through the soles of her shoes, comforting.

She slices the onion.
Wet, translucent petals fall
onto the cutting board.
The greater the sting
the more carefully she guides the knife.
Heaped on the cutting board—piles
of perfectly sliced vegetables, an edible mosaic.
She inhales the sizzling onion scent;
her body moves—jazz.

You can find her in the kitchen
when she returns.
She is smiling, inquiring.
He does not say, "Do you forgive me? So easily?"
He says, "How was your day?"
Then, they sit together,
lift their forks,
talking smaller and smaller.

Moon Walk

Twenty-one, carrying my baby boy
in one of these front-facing packs
that hug the child close,
but let your arms fly free,
I walked to see a late show
at the one-dollar theater.

The film wasn't billed as *scary*,
but there were moments, like when
she lost her child in the store for just a moment,
then when she cut her finger but didn't notice at first,
her consciousness suspended, waiting for her lover to call.

The child snored; I was alone, munching on
extra-buttered popcorn that later would
have me out of bed three times
during the night to get water.

On the walk home under the sodium lights
of the parking lot, my own spotlight, I considered
not going home to the man-boy who since the birth of our child
had become so much more mine to tend.

I passed house after soggy house, until
I reached our bright white mailbox,
a wedding present from my Mom.
Hand painted lilacs, a symbol,
she said, of love.

Approaching our house, the boy squirmed,
his fisted hand opening and closing on my index finger,
a kind of baby Morse code I couldn't crack.

I let my head fall back to view the stars
whose names I never learned.

As I rearranged his blanket,
secured it with the crook of my arm,
I thought of buying a baby-books on stargazing,
one of those board books that are also good for gnawing,
then I turned and walked away from the house,
to walk just a little while longer, collecting moonlight, feeling my breath —
catch, hold — release.
Wearing loneliness,
a fine-beaded shawl.

Epiphany of a young mother

Silk eyes closed, new-born rubs his face
against my breast, more quickly
as his frustration builds.

He grasps
and sucks what
his balled-up fists can find to hold.

I want to sink
 into the cracks of the sofa
with the lost change.

A boy once promised
to climb in the barrel
and lift up his shirt,
if I did it first.

A clever trick.
I didn't know:
there's no shame for boys
in barrel games.

Gym class, training bras,
Names inked blue on white T-shirts.

Tits.
Melons. Jugs. Boobs.
Look at the rack on that one!
Round. Oiled. Forbidden.

Now, this.
Little fingers reach upward,
A stifled cry, his head moves side to side.

Cracks of overuse
are easily endured because, after all,
his eyes are soft as pollen,
his hands are petals, opening again and again,
his head drenches my palm with sweat,
and though he looks as though he'd like to eat his own face,
he calms the instant his hunger is fed.

In this lost change moment, the world tilts.

No shame, after all,
in barrel games.

If he doesn't get home soon

She folds fruit-of-the-looms
the way grandmother taught her to fold, tucks
corners of bed sheets under,
perfect love triangles.

Fuckin' prick
she says loud,
wishing for a cigarette,
a rum 'n coke,
to set the mood
as she swears this time
she aint gonna back down,
gonna tell him
he's been fuckin' around
and she's better than that,
knows better than that.

She thinks she'll do it.
Thinks she'll tell him
he's a beer-gut, self-centered
shell of the man
he used to be and she's got big plans.
Baby, you aint in 'em.

But, if he doesn't get home soon,
she's probably going to accept his next apology.
Anger always comes first,
then fear.

Love

Proper poets will not use the word,
though it is their chief concern.
Cliché to name it, unless
you're young, 19, and cumming
on the roof of a Datsun 280Z
in the pitch black desert while coyote howls
at a sky full of stars, a neon moon.

Now, young mother, suckling her child
while balancing a plate of spaghetti on her right
hand and a college textbook on her left
cannot recall it,
cannot recall the sound of that coyote's howl.

The quintessential sin.
Even Miller's John Proctor,
noble and wise, was doomed
to commit it, as 280Z did.
But how did she become an Elizabeth?
In the distance, a howl.

To keep it she will buy
nipple rings on ebay and learn to be
a connoisseur of pornography,
but in the darkness, handcuffed,
she knows that it is not any of these trappings,
and it is hers for the taking.
If only she'd take it,
and leave him.

Ladies, love!

Deep greens and blues remind me of walking
hand-in-hand over railroad tracks to nowhere,
turning and walking back to where we started.
Remind me of kissing you,
not like kissing a man — like kissing every woman.

Remember when we took turns rubbing each other's back?
How we sketched our house plan?
We were twelve. How we believed
we'd grow up and live together
with our husbands and babies?

I washed your feet.
I combed your hair.

The air on the Pacific Ocean is cold in November,
but I was warmed by your daring,
jumped the waves, with you.

Ladies, love!
We are all of us wanting to be understood.
We are ugly. We are beautiful.
What's the difference?

We are blooming and dying and blooming again.
Ladies, love!
Each other.
Wash her feet.
Comb her hair.

Pecan Pie

Seed pods in the mortar,
cardamom, the word,
tickles my lips.
Elbow-grinding with marble pestle,
I pull three cinnamon sticks
from that spice jar we bought in Santa Fe,
and laugh at how we were then:
a short laugh, abruptly ended
because you broke my heart and I am
alive, but homeless.

Crust ephemeral, flaky,
of course pecans, corn syrup,
and eggs. It's 2 A.M.
I'm baking a pie!

Sitting on the porch
in the warm night air,
cinnamon fingers
turn the pages of a paperback novel.
I heave a lonely, somewhat satisfied sigh,
waiting for the pie to be done, for the day to rise.

A grape. A worm. A kaleidoscope.

I've noticed the way
you cover you mouth.
Such a gesture signals insecurity,
or so I've been told.

I know it's not enough to simply say,
"Don't cover your mouth" or
"You have a beautiful smile. Why hide it?"
So, I say nothing,
only watch, worried.

You used to always be climbing into my lap,
making sound effects with your legos,
"Pew-pew-pew — He shooting you."
You taught me how to marvel
at not the universe, but the pebbles of it:
a grape, a worm, a kaleidoscope.
If I'd ever known these things, I'd long forgot.

Hand over your mouth,
I fear you are forgetting, and I want
to tie this poem around your finger.
A grape. A worm. A kaleidoscope.

What I Learned From The Rain

Yesterday,
mid-week drag,
reluctant spring had me down,
pissed about the undone dishes,
dirty floor—child of mine.

What looked like the ground flowers
we buy and light before dark every July, flashed
across his computer screen, while he clicked
his mouse and talked into a tiny mic
to god knows who—how old—where?

I'm going for a walk, I said,
reluctant, like spring at first and pouty too,
I plodded along under a dull sky,
thinking in circles.

Drops of rain came down, a few at first,
on top of my head,
then on my shoulders,
then sliding down my face like cold tears.
I'd walked the long route winding through
familiar streets, down and around the lake.

Half way up the steepest hill,
sun broke through, lighting my path home.
I picked my chin up off the sidewalk,
saw the rainbow doing her backbend across the
sky.
Quickening my pace, watching my breath
move in-out, and again, wind lifted and tossed
my hair. I skipped a few steps, jumped—
yes, jumped—two feet together,
into a puddle. Then the next, and the next.

Home, which felt like home again,
I entered, revived, lauging.

Pay Day

Being pay day, I could afford the movie,

the popcorn that looked over-large in your lap.

I could afford new shoes for you and me,

cart full of groceries, and to pick up developed photos

from your tenth birthday party.

32 prints, 10 that were worth keeping,

found filed alphabetically by your last name.

I thumbed through them,

surprised to come across a photo of me

I'd forgotten I let you take.

Blurry, taken too close, you can see every blemish,

every patch of apigmentation, even the

chicken pox scar on my right forehead.

But I am laughing like I'd forgotten I could.

Eyes squinted, cheeks, blushed,

full-faced laugh-roar.

Obstinate, young

He pretty much gives me the look every day now.
Are-you-my-mother?
But not like the little bird in the book.
Disdainful.

I asked him to put away
laundry I cared to fold.
He wanted to know:
What's the point?
When you're just going to wear them again?

Because I said so.
Saying what I never thought I would,
as he stomped up the stairs,
slammed his bedroom door,
I snuck in a soft I love you
he didn't or wouldn't hear.

I checked to find my feet still planted on the floor,
reminded myself I had my turn too,
to be obstinate, young.

He's grown dark fuzz above his upper lip.
We wear the same size shoe.
If it weren't for morning,
when he wakes drowsy and sits, leaning against me
on the couch while I read, the dog sleeping at our feet,
I might lose my patience or worse —
my mind-- about these matters.

Sunset In That Lonesome Valley

C'mere, he said.
My heart is a dust bowl and you
look like a tall glass of water,
a bud about to bloom.

Californication played on the radio.
We'd been driving for nine hours already
when we stopped to watch the sun set in that lonesome valley.
C'mere, he said,
but it's the sunset I'll never forget.

Mat

Black mat firm and worked

soft by years of splayed fingers and toes.

In the rush to get these boxes

out of the truck and the rain,

this mat, she left propped against the sliding glass door

that opens to what can only be

a container garden on a concrete condo patio.

A shadow of the ten by ten plot left behind.

She will go in search of it soon,

because she will need it to help her breathe

through this separation between desire and truth.

She will wash the oil and dirt that the rain did not

with soap and warm water and hang this mat to dry

in the sun that is tomorrow's forecast.

Love letter

It's been raining for fifteen days.
It's time to put summer's clothes away,
bring the wool sweaters out—I'm shivering.
This autumn, I am throwing out your clothes,
the leaves in black plastic bags.
I realize now you won't be by to pick them up.
You won't be bringing candles on stormy days when lights flicker.
On Halloween, I'll place jack-o-lanterns on the lawn
to keep the spirits out.

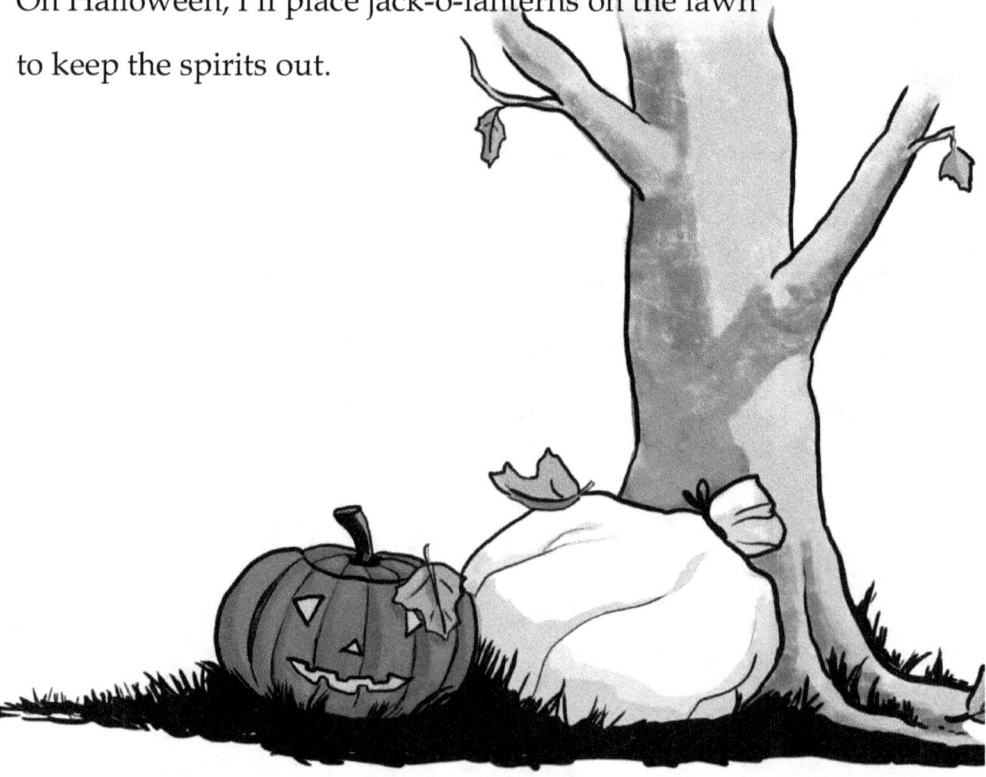

Bankrupt

No television judge, his voice cracks

into a glass of clear water

that he gulps, saying, "any creditors

here in this matter?"

White walls hold their breath, feet on faux marble tiles

stop tapping, listen to the sound of debt papers

clamoring to be released

into the scheme of things and paperweights.

"This meeting is concluded."

Like he does this every day.

I emerge with papercuts: thinner,

older, melancholic,

bankrupt, ready.

Balboa Park

Watching this line of ants
run across the crack in the concrete,
I think, Robert Frost did it:
Why can't I?
But this doesn't sit well--
pen hovers over the blank page,
neck tightens.

I'm breaking down, I know,
so I try to write about strolling
yesterday through Balboa Park,
but when I look over the lines
I've written, there's not an image
or a hint of that wonder,
aside from the title on the page,
only some musings on desire
and a mention of tongue-kissing.

There was that squirrel,
the one with the crazy long
legs that leapt and crept,
surprised our jittery, nut-munching expectations
so we laughed out loud; the so close hawks--counted four--
waiting for the sky to fall; the chime
of the way up there Spanish mosaic design bell tower;
the trying hard, we're-new-at-this,
children's swing band.

You pointed out the bright mango
couple dancing in the concert backdrop
and we made up a story to explain them.
.
We strolled across the string-light
bridge over the--surprise--dense,

green, rising--freeway.

The tea garden: closed.
The museum: closed.
The botanical garden: closed.

We walked unprotected from ourselves
in the warm bright air,
wishing the next airplane
that flew too close
across the swimming pool blue sky
could carry the hungry liars
who live in us far-far away.

It wasn't even you I wanted to kiss,
but petals of you and me dropped
and blown, expecting
to reach the bay.

Loneliness

Naked from hip to heel,
I sat, chin propped on knees,
feeling the caress of a blue silk button-up, chosen
because I missed you and it had been one of *those* days.

My phone buzzed.
I jittered like a host
before her guests arrive at your OMW.

When you rose to go, after sex, a little sleep,
I mimicked sleep,
listened to the rustle of your slacks, click of your belt,
minor squeak as you put on each shoe.

I imagined the scene when you returned to your home.
She left the light on, as always,
a note on the table.
Had she written out the word *love* or abbreviated it with
a symbol?
Did she draw an arrow piercing clean through?

I slept montage dreams, then woke cold,
unable to recall any particulars.
Rising to make coffee, my legs ached (too little water, I thought),
my belly growled (light dinner).
I boiled water for oatmeal, took butter out of the fridge,
then pulled the honey off the shelf.

The kettle whistle sounded like howling.
Fear, without pronouncement, rattled me,
and my panicked heart sought ritual in making his school lunch.
Loaf of bread.
Jar of peanut butter.
Strawberry jam.

I called upstairs,
"Son! Wake up! It's time to shower."
Resumed: one side peanut butter,
one side jam.
Cut in two, placed in the zipper seal bag,
that bag placed in the bag with the honey-crisp
apple, the kettle-cooked chips.

The whole lunch placed in his backpack,
I wondered what my life will come to when
he is no longer around to make sandwiches for,
when he is making his own or someone else's,
in his own house, his own kettle howling?
What new ritual will make me feel that,
for someone, I am needed?

Even in Silence

Mid-February,
tripping into spring,
late-night outdoor lounging begins,
changing my soundtrack for evening.

Neighbors watching crowded TV screens,
banging dinner's pots and pans.
No time to place them
noiselessly in cupboards.

Fighting young lovers,
their anger urgent, exploding
into loud, certain words.

Cat rustles in the oleander.
Socialite frogs mingle at their nightly cocktail party.
Wind chimes signal something is coming;
something is always coming our way.

The continuous freeway sounds of passing on and on and on
lulls the neighborhood to sleep.
The night bird howls loneliness;
there is no silence, even in silence.

Enchanted Valley, 2004

Pushing past thimbleberries and ferns,
ancient, towering cedars holding me in,
not to mention the persistent burn in my shoulders,
I arrive at a clapboard chalet in the middle of a rock-green valley.

Washing socks in the river, I take my time,
rinsing and rubbing until
every patch of ground in dirt and dried blood
breaks free from the cotton weave,
follows the river's current.

Crouched by that cold, blue river's edge,
each inhalation drives evergreens, dark and floating
into the valley between my ribs,
where they expand into light.

Exhalations send slate grey ghouls
up from the pit in my stomach, scurrying
up the towering stone walls
that hold us in.

A mass of birch trees remind me of poetry, specifically Frost,
when, my son approaches, riding piggy-back,
from where his aunt took him out scouting for beasts.
They laugh in tandem,
bounce across the rocks toward me.

I put down my pen to boil water,
prepare macaroni and cheese for three.

Open Space

I attempt to catapult my broken mind
by trekking into open space,
not swaggering, but charging unfamiliar trail.
Blossoms trumpet spring and forge determination,
rival leafless, serene winter garments.

At the zenith, a burnt orange fire road, plush with new grass,
creates a background for a wild flower collage, a frame even.

Breathe dirty air, wet earth scent.
Blue wild irises break stale thought,
egg-yolk poppies feed hungry eyes,
as the deep green quiet pulls attention to subtler sound.

To say I've hit my stride is to simplify
this fantastic lactic roll,
past sticky monkey, up inclines:
rock, dirt, twisted roots.

Lizard skitters across the path.
Hawk cries overhead.
Brown cow chews her cud behind the electric fence.
I smile, prepare
for another incline.

Until You

A stray cat, until you

walked into that stray-cat bar,

holding the moon in your arms,

part piper, part prophet, part Phineas.

Happy to fend and scrape,

heart pumped full of tequila and NO

until you, with the moon in your arms, smiled.

Unaware as you smile-talked, that you were

holding the moon--a miracle! Until you,

I looked up and could not see

the constellations for the stars.

Until you, No.

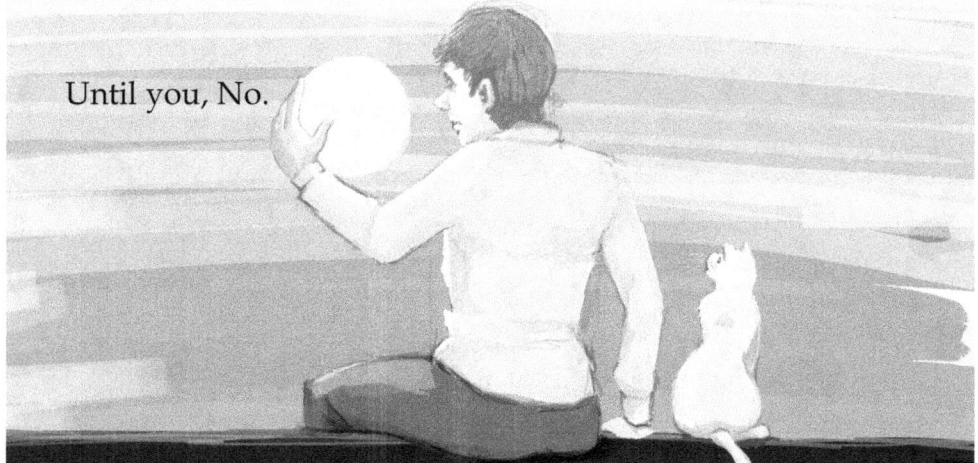

Poppies in May

Tall, pale green awkward stems,

one propped up with a stake--stretched thin--

like an addict,

but ah...the plump oval bud bursts open,

the blood red petals

darkest at the center, edges paler

reveal themselves rice paper thin--

Stamen and petals covered--

fine, soft, yellow dust.

In two days or three the petals will fall.

Beauty lies dormant for another year.

The Sculptor

Against snow-capped mountains
firs huddle gregarious,
limb-arms inviting all to linger
on the sun-warmed rocks,
where the sculptor works without tiring.

Without ceasing, without hesitation,
moving down-across-through-
energy rushing, spilling forward
and onward. Blue sculptor,
fresh and cold.

On the sand bar, we are bears,
our tired paws renewed by the sculptor,
wet and bright.

Ode to the Avocado

You contain perfect green wonder,
so easily yielding to my spoon.

Delight, when you are ripe, to cut open.
Disappointment if my impatience tempts me
to peek too soon, or if, in daily-haste,
I miss the signs of readiness.

I loved you before he spoke the words, "I'm sorry,"
eyes focused on his untied canvas sneakers.

I loved you before I fell out of love with him
and into love with *him*,
before *he* fell out of love with me.

Heart-sized.
Oh, avocado!

I'm taking this slimy brown pit,
suspending it on toothpicks
on the rim of this jar of water
where the sunlight will collect and refract.

I'll be checking on you everyday,
praying you'll root and grow
so I can transplant you
and have hearts to spare someday.

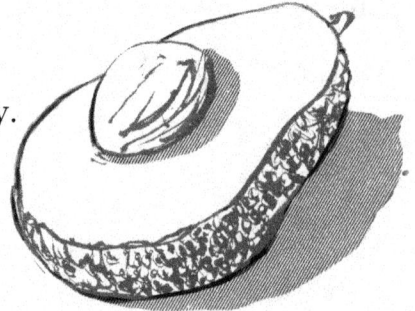

Linger, love.

Whether you and I observe--
lying in the cool grass of evening,
your leg crossing mine--
my fingers brushing your palm,
the moon will glow.

Whether we take that switchback
trail at dawn, laughing into the open space
around us and between us
under the moon's light-blanket,
that stream is playing its part.
Eternal concert, we sometimes care to listen to.

Oh love! Linger here
even when--especially when--
I alone observe the moon,
stroll singular beside the chattering stream.

Language

I call you
love-eyes, bright mind,
the first of epithets
in our secret love-language.
Where words become you and me,
and we delight in this word-play,
soul syntax, plus it seems
the future will not be abbreviated.

Descriptions fall short
of experience. I am left to
meander in metaphor.

A fortune cookie
with only one word hidden inside--yes.
The part of the wave that touches my shore
again and again. Skipping class,
but learning more.
The used book I bought as much for
the notes scribbled in the margins as for
the poetry inside.
A brand new pen that was a splurge
as far as pens go, like the one I'm using now,
thinking of how you are so much delight...
A kiwi berry.
A certain slant of light.
An evolution of language and, in turn,
a shift in how my eyes interpret signals.

A Good Snow

A good snow,
switches off our hum and buzz.
Traffic crawls
or doesn't move at all.
Muffled voices swirl up
with the chimney smoke, to become
stark, silent sound in the bright, white sky.

A good snow,
switches off our get and go,
tuning in the white, noiseless Wonder.

The art of snow angels:
Getting up without wrinkling your wings,
tattering your skirt.

The art of snow balls:
How to pack and throw while laughing
so bold it hurts.

A good snow turns me into a mad igloo builder
who will not give in,
even when only the stars remain to guide her,
opening her to the echo of
art for art,
for art.

Like the first kiss

Our lips touched as I dropped you off last night.
A shock of electricity sprang up between us,
like a storm coming or taking out
a dryer full of overdone towels.

When I picked you up four hours later,
still thinking of that first kiss,
I couldn't wait to watch you
declothe in the lamplight,
pet the eager dogs,
pick up your library book
where you'd left off.

You started it with a hand,
a kiss to the nape of my neck.
You unfolded me,
shook me like fresh sheets,
took care to make all the corners fit.
We floated on our backs
all the way
across the lake.

You folded me up again.
I opened my book,
stepped in where I'd left off.
We drifted far, far apart.

You read some pages,
did a crossword.
We shut off our lamps,
walked alone into our dreams.

Advice From A Swing Set

We used to sometimes sit on
black rubber seats of swing sets,
talking in confidence,
bending, then straightening our legs,
make-shift rocking chairs.

Other times we would scissor our bodies
together on one swing, alternating
the task of pumping legs.
A slow moving—
laughing—crab creature.

We would sit side by side,
pumping and pushing
to gain a swing motion
that might take us upside down this time.
But always there was that click
at the top of the chain,
indicating you'd get no higher.

We'd go as high as we could,
then at the count of
1-2-3—
push off from the seat,
fly through the air,
aiming for a controlled landing
like Nadia on TV.

www.ingramcontent.com/pod-product-compliance
Lightning Source LLC
Chambersburg PA
CBHW070552300426
44113CB00011B/1881